Oceans, Tears and Realization

By: Ali Al-Arithy

For you,

It's okay to feel that way, no matter what it is, know that you are not alone and eventually you will have the answer.

I learned it shows up in the most unexpected places.

I am here for you, that's certain.

-With words forever.

Ali Al-Arithy

Table of Contents:

Oceans:

Tears:

4

Realizations:

Oceans:

It's happened already

I think it's beautiful when someone loves you,
When someone could make you feel something you haven't felt before.
When someone can decide for you, even though you haven't even
thought about what you would have decided on.
A tremendous love, one that needs no explanation or gander, it can be
read without sight and felt without touch.
It can be transfused into the air itself and you are able to take it all in,
And keep taking it in as if it never runs out.
I think it's beautiful when someone loves you, did you know it's
already happened?

I hope that makes you happy

I have a question?

What makes you happy?

Did you think of it?

I'll give you another second?

How about now?

Whatever it is, I hope it makes you happy.
I hope it gives you the vitality that you lost when you thought they were a part of you.
The part that you gave so much nutrition to, that you forgot to give anything left to yourself. Remember that moment you expressed how proud you were, that you could give yourself to yourself without a second thought. I hope that makes you happy.

9

Oceans

Looking at the ocean doesn't feel the same anymore.

The first thoughts as the water seeps into the sand, is you.

And the first word that is uttered is your name in the wind bringing you back to me.

The first body movement is my hands holding my face as it gets heavy in confusion.

And the first sound is what could be your voice being taken by the undertow.

The first sight blurry, as if rain uncontrivable on glass with curiousness of the beauty on the other side.

And the first step away from what I thought I needed, from what I thought I couldn't live without. And in that thought I realized that this step is all I need to realize the importance that I am to myself.

Say it, first

The air in my lungs is faint.

There is nothing left but a hollow space for what is supposed to be for you.

I don't feel you palpitating, I don't feel your knocking, even though I would let you in every time.

Your necessary thoughts could have been the strings that held you inside of me, instead they have become dead branches that are brittle to the touch.

What if

What if I told you that I am in love with you?
But not just with you but your face when you talk about the things
that make you humble.
And when you think you chuckle but you actually giggle at the things
you only find humorous.
And when you laugh so much your lips disappear as they stick to your
teeth.
And you think your flawed hair style is actually one part of you that I
look forward to.
And when your nose flares in a solace that radiates your passion
behind the words that you stand behind.
And your mind, when it carries words on the back of words without
having limits on what may sometimes sound endless.
And that's when I knew I was in love with you, when it seemed like
nothing that was wrong mattered, and what mattered never seemed
as important.

Raindrops

My fingers are so tired.

They are tired because I keep forcing them to stay away.

I force them to train the muscles and the fibers not to cling on the softest breaches of your mind.

I don't understand, they don't understand how leaving me blind in the darkness, or rather I think it's the darkness, but that's what it feels like. A happy place full of the worst manipulation I have ever seen.

The blind fold, your fingers, I force myself to pull them off of my skin and still they come with a stronger grip.

Leave me, leave me alone because my eye sight is not your eye sight, let me fixate on the things that make all of this worth it.

And stop controlling the tears that run down my face and leave my fingers alone because that's the only way I can catch them.

Confined, confined space that I can barely move and your fingers lock into mine and I finally feel the slight hope that you may have turned a different leaf.

Are you better? Can I give more than my fingers and maybe my shoulder so you can tell me who hurt you, and why you feel the need to use your fingers for the destruction that you think is "nothing but love for you". Love has a sense of humor, the cloud that is above me is not spewing raindrops but hail that is mesmerizing from a window on a Saturday evening with the warm coffee that you caress with your hands.

And through that hail storm of all the sadness you make me feel out of obligation, I reach out these fingers in hopes you will hold them.

10:28pm

What is so special about that hour and minute?
I know you can tell time; what time is it now? One-minute passes and my mind can't take the concept that I can never get that minute again.

So, I write words, a plethora of words so I can use the seconds wisely and record these words so I may feel like I am using my time to make my thoughts seen. And another minute goes by and I can only think of sleeping but instead I am writing as another minute passes and now, now it sounds like it is going nowhere, where am I going with this?

Oh, I remember how excited I became when time was able to give me the anticipation and the assurance that I will see you. And after I saw you, it gave me the urgency to feel your heartbeat when you would talk about the plans that you have to make yourself better.

The happiest time for me is seeing your eyes glow with desire and having the glasses on your face enhance the glow, blinding me with happiness. You see when they say time doesn't stop, they lied. It does stop when you make the conscious effort of living in the moment and space that you are in. Right now.

This moment you are living in, it is because you are learning something new.
A new that you weren't expecting but you fixate, it lets you become aware of what you have or could have and it helps you connect your discoveries with your dreams and now you have a plan.
Eight minutes passed by, they passed by and now I am wondering if I said enough words in those eight minutes that it took me to write these words to define the simplicity of how your interaction with time is a violating relationship and you should perceive it any way you deem appropriate.

A relationship raw and full of all the honesty that will make you realize how valuable your time is.

14

In my opinion, it is a construction of the phases of the day and time makes you realize how much space you have left. Spend it with you, spend it with the only person that you can call on anytime in the night, especially at 3am.

Would you wake up for me, would you wake up for the only time my mind seems to understand itself?

Would you consider my emotions when they are the most fruitful? Nectarines can't compare to all the sweetness, giving me a sweet rush of agony.
Would you consider waking up?

Here it is

My desire

Take what's left of the excruciating need to feel like I could be. Part of anything that you love.

Take

My subconscious

Take it away, to a place I wouldn't think of because it has been the one thing I can stay without.

Take

My Dreams

Take them with you when you follow your dreams, I hope they make you keep reaching.

Take

The night skies

Take it so it stays in that beautiful hour where all your fears are the things that become vulnerable.

Take

The roads

Take the road that we used to step into without incessantly thinking about the what if's, because you held my hand closely, reassuring me that the dead branches on the ground make the most beautiful music.

Take

Manipulating

Take the manipulating gestures and inclinations of the people that come into your life because that could be the only way to understand what you should be weary of.

Take

That something

Take that something that allows you to wake up in the middle of the night and not have it be a bad dream or tirelessness from that day that potentially could have been the last day to your sanity. A moment that you can stare into the empty ceiling and think of all the ways you're able to find beauty that you are meant to find.

Give

Give me just a fraction of your time.

A decent word that I could find while others remain searching.

A constant acknowledgement that my worth is just as equal as yours when you are most confident.

A reason, like the one reason you have that wakes you up in the morning, and I am not talking about your job.

Give me a desire to be passionate about, the way I exhale when my anxiety takes over.

Give my subconscious a reason to love my fears without letting them take over.

Give me dreams I can write about the next morning because the detail could be a potential novel.
Give that night sky a date and remember it forever.
Give me a map I can figure out, and let your love be the compass.

Give me manipulation, but only manipulate my worries the ones that stop my voice from explaining myself.
Give me something, something I don't have to explain, and no matter what question comes up, I will always have the answer.

18 words

When I
want to write a word
where I don't stumble over other words
I write your name.

89 degrees

The clicking of a type writer,
A glass being filled half way,
A candle swaying in a room where there is no wind,
And your hum in that silent room,
That's my favorite sound.

3389 Greenfield Rd

Coffee with you,
In the evening time.
Is like having the conversation,
That I had with you the first time,
I knew I met,
You

Coffee

Sunday morning,

I woke up to not the alarm intended for Monday morning, I woke up to the sound of a fan, humming a serenade that validated how alive I really am.

How dreams are just a temporary escape that feel like seconds from the hour you place your head on the pillow, to the hour that you wake up.
4:30....is too early.... or maybe too late, no it's definitely late. I'm going to be late, too late to remember all of the dream.
You're going away.
I remember you happy, I saw your smile in the mirror and I was floating away from you staring in the mirror smiling... like you didn't do it often.

The world around me shifted into a forest full of illuminated spider webs, being held by the extensions of branches, I think Christmas came early. I stood there in front of you holding my happy face and that was the first time I sinned in greed as if you were only mine.

It shifted again and now it was sand and an ocean, I walked into the ocean knowing full well it is my worst fear. I needed to show you how far I will go...and you watched me sink while we had the same facial expression.
And the moment before waking up, I called out to you from the balcony of a hotel room burning, as it absorbed all of the colors from the sunset that scorched the side of the building and that balcony was where you didn't say anything back. That's when I woke up Sunday morning to not the alarm intended for Monday morning, I woke to the sound of a fan, humming a serenade that validated how alive I really am.

And love...

And love...made me want to show my happiness to everyone that
never mattered.
I wanted to be a coward to its oppression, only I craved and begged to
being submissive to its dominance.
I wanted nothing but to fulfill your wish to only feel accepted.
To feel like my acceptance is the key to all the doors that you keep
closed because you told me that, that key that I created out of the
years of mending was not the right fit for any of the doors you keep
locked.

I want to let go, but then I think of the surety of gravity and its
attempt to keep me grounded so I don't float to a reminder that I am
not sure I can get away from.
Boundless,
contemplation on a conversation that I never had with you, but
wanted to give you all the right words so I write the words on my skin
just so I don't forget hot deeply imbedded you are in my chest.

22

Spring on March 30th

The sun after the rain
The sad that goes away
The subtly of waves in a puddle
The satisfying smell of rush in the city
The smell of your skin when we sin
The store that is still open at 3am
The sight of you in the kitchen in the morning
The significant silence in a crowded room that you are not a part of
The smile that made me fall in love with the rain, yours actually
That Sunday when it rained again, was the day I went outside and
challenged the rain with the tears that tore me just so I can feel like
everyone else.

"Whose fault is it"

The same time last year there was a coldness that you could only feel when your hands feel the numbness of dry ice.
Like the little hope you carry in your palm, and you cup that hope like fire, even though there is nothing around to blow it out.

The same time last year I also felt happier, happier to be in the skin I am in and the mindset that I would walk countries for you...I know its drastic, okay you get what I mean.
Last year at this time I felt like something was going to happen, what will happen will dictate our positions in the world and that will indefinitely be the answer that I have been dreading without ever feeling dread when it came to you.

This time last year, it rained and I remember that because I remember dates and times ever since I met you.
I remember hours and minutes because they are the same numbers that you use for dates, and with the date, giving the month, day and the year will give me the pleasure of keeping these dates because you were worth it.

You were worth the moments that were the most impactful to me.

In March last year, I thought I would hear good news, news that I have been anticipating and hoping for because I felt this endless wait would never be in the time it was supposed to be.

Last year, I didn't think that I would ever not hear from you again.

Tears:

Tears

I want to see you in the day light.

Where the sun has no choice but to forcefully shine.

At the sight of you, not because there is a forced

sunrise that makes no sense without your eyes when they open.

And when you close those eyes at the end of the day.

 I can't help but to dream of them until the next sunrise.

Breathe

You can only see it in front of you when its below 7.22C or 45 degrees F.

And just because you can't see it, it doesn't mean that it's not there.

It can block the simple steps in front of you.

Your breath can fill an entire space around you.

When you enter a room, it is your breathing that helps people understand who you are.

The understanding is deafening,

I figured out what your lungs are capable of, they can expand with limit, and for some reason when it comes to you being you, you are limitless.

If I can see your breath, I know it forces itself to stay in the same space that your body is in.

You breathe, life into me and the ones that surround you will feel like there isn't enough air when you're not there.

Keep breathing.

Take

I am not sure if I were ever on my side, I seemed vibrant and accurate when I took on other scenarios.

They were effortless and my attention, all of my attention seemed to seep and repair all that has been broken. And when I was shattered, I never looked inside and allowed myself to heal, I expected it to come from something else, someone else. Anyone that could communicate in a language that I can understand. Even in the language of silence, a language I was fluent in.

Like a white noise that I know is there but I never understand which direction it is coming from.
Or that ringing in your ear that happens randomly and you can't help but to become a deer in headlights for a few seconds.
Have you noticed that you don't think about anything in those few seconds but that noise?

Just like those few seconds that you forget about all the pain, you are healing yourself, you are realizing who and what is that noise, that sound of hope that your pieces are mending, mending not like they used to be but mending into the miraculous person that you will become, and only you can allow it.

Reflect

There's a time when you will feel it.

You know that feeling when you fall down, but you find no reason to get up, and you just keep falling because that's what happened the first time.

That first fall made you realize that aggression that comes over you when you have not gained the right words to slowly pick yourself up again.

Words that are used to compromise and build the last resort to your complete happiness, your feet are tree trunks.

What does it mean to be hostile to yourself?

Was it him or her or them?

That one person that could have used all their emotions and to you that person feels like four people overbearing you with empty words. I want to tell you, you're the tree that is admired often, the tree that will hug you back, the tree that allows shade and makes wind its bitch.

You're the tree that stands against the lightening and gives refuge to the bird with the broken wing.

You're immense and because your roots were once a seed that fell, my confidence in you is better than yesterday and it can't be measured.

You have always been my happiness, you have always been me. You are important.

I missed myself, I missed you

I have yet to figure out what it meant when you said "I need to focus
on myself".

But you never said it, you made it simple, clear is a better word.

Or maybe the word revelation, it's appropriate.

You made it seem like the words that I opened you up with yesterday
are like the button that you accidentally push and then it sends you to
the trap room of a house you're not supposed to be in.

Sometimes I wish you would say something...anything...any form of
communication that you deem worthy...any sound that could hint
your fascination with something else.

You could have prevented this silence, just by uncovering the truth
that you use as a reason to force yourself to love you.

Do you love you, do you think of you as another person?

A person that could have been neglected to be honest with the truth.
Now I am not saying the truth is me, but what I'm trying to say is that
I carry some truth. I revealed your weakness as your strength, and
your strength as the motivation that you need, now.

I hope you understand every confusion, and I hope you allow what
and who to come in with ease and not an obstruction that you use as
an excuse or a reason not to allow love in. You know, you need it,
right?

You need that immediate feeling of love, one that is accessible, but
never treat it as a convenience.

It will be there, I learned it is abundant and no matter how much you
may think I waste from that love I want you to know I will always
have it for you and it will always flow into you consistent. But you
made a choice, you chose the silence.

4:17am

Monday morning, I couldn't feel you like I did on Sunday night.
The morning has brought the sensible discovery that I still feel lonely.
That I still feel like strength doesn't have to hide behind the
vulnerable face that I can compare to what I feel inside.
It's not the first thing in the morning, when you have been awake in
my mind all night.
I turn the fan on in 17-degree weather because the silence haunts me
with your voice, and in the cold night when I can't control what I hear
in my head.
 I don't know how, but it keeps me up at night.
It keeps me up to the next hour until the sun decides to come up.
Can I sleep now?

I can't hear you

My heart breaks every day when I hear your name in a room full of silence.

I am glad I can finally hear it.

There were so many ways I could have made you understand my love.

I could have made you fall in love with me if I wanted, even though I never knew how.

All I did was fall into a passion that I never gave myself.

I could never think of many ways I could have given it to myself but I will still find a way how.

Leave me here

Take me back to that wonderful place you called love.
That is what I could have said but stopped myself because you were the one that didn't say it back.
I let you in every time, I let you eat with me, in the same table that we discussed the things that didn't work out but never the things that could have easily turned my day into a better one.
You stayed up with me when I was sick, even though I had no signs of sickness and no ability to realize that it was all in my head. You see me nervous and out of breath but instead you told me to "keep going". I never could look you in the eye, even though I knew this truth that could for the life of me, save me.
You were that plant, let me specific that cactus, so good to look at and can with stand being without water but I knew I couldn't reach out to you.
Sunsets you made seem like the most beautiful scenes and then decide to suffocate me with your arm of doubt around my neck, you kept telling me how good I am at not being good enough.
You made me realize that without you I can never move forward in my successes because they are not mine to keep, so you tell me you need them back because they are creations that I should not be confident about.
You hovered over me, when you said that you were confident in me to make a fraction of a decision that could take me to a better place.
You locked my mouth shut when I needed to defend myself from the harm of the pellets that come from the mouths of those that manifest their envy.
Ocean, remember when you said the ocean was my downfall because all of the dreams that I worked so hard to make true, are nothing but subtle whirlpools of immaturity.
Take me back to that wonderful place called love, were you ever going to take me there, does it even exist, does it fall between an intersection that I may have passed ten times but your manipulation has been pristine every time?

33

Take me back to that wonderful place called love, has that place been only you?

Is it your house? Is it an alleyway that holds the graffiti so explicit, that keeps those lines of my anxiety out of order, because you never figured out how to make a house a home?

Leave me here, with this watch so I can tell time, so I can wake up on the right side of the bed.

Next to the empty water bottle that I already pissed because I woke up twenty times.

Just leave me here.

All the things I could have said

When I have so much to say, there is a voice in my head that says "shut up".
And for some reason when that voice tells me to shut up, I can't help but stay silent. It wants me to anticipate the shit that could easily come out of the ones that were a part of my day.

You want to know what else it says, "you can do it", and when that voice says that I can do it. I can stop the train which is your thoughts and I can easily pull the lever that could curve that flow of words into another direction, because right now my time is worth it.
I make it sound like I have multiple voices in my head but its only one, one distinct voice that I use. Sometimes it's too quiet, that while I try to sleep, I like to pretend that I hear the roar of a fan in my face so I can feel like I am alive.

"Seek help", seek another voice a comfortable objective voice that can say all the words and all the resolve that I contemplated every time, 97 times actually and I sit there and come up with all the reason that I am the best therapist for myself.

When I say "I am not crazy", I'm not and now you are thinking that I am because I am using the word "crazy" and the words "I am not" in the same sentence with a hint of shrill in my voice as it shakes, I know you are judging me.
Judgement, when I say that word I think of god, with a sledgehammer instead of a gavel, because its dramatic that way. Smashing the podium that is your perception, that I used to declare my sanity and to defend myself from this voice that holds me back from what I am capable of.

I am capable, capable of so much that wonder is inescapable, of the love that I hold back because I forgot to give it to myself. I forget that existing in this body and realizing that it needs love too is enough. It's enough to grasp that me being allowed to let myself breath is my choice. I choose to breath and when I exhale, I will tell you all the things that I could have muttered when I never had a voice because it felt like my mind had a foot and that foot was forced on my vocal cords.

Like my tongue split in half from constant razor-sharp words, that form, from my frustration and if you heard those words, they would have given you the deepest of wounds. And if I kissed you, my tongue would introduce you to a prison you could never be free from.

I could have said a lot of things and I kept them to myself because inflicting myself first makes me immune to the many apples in Eden that I could have tasted when you presented the garden to me, it was never a place I wanted to be in. And that voice is the last one I hear before I sleep in the burial ground that is my bed, the burial ground where I leave my day all behind. And then that voice says "you did it", and in that dream I am suffocating and all I can do is watch myself.

Give me all your love

Give me enough so I can exist in this world without questioning its judgment.

Fill my coffee mug in the morning because I would love for it to give me the motivation for today.

Make it visible when I put on my glasses, because you know I will be sure that it's there when I have to take them off eventually.

Write it down on a paper and shred it up, I will find a way to put it back together.

Point at it, in a place without light pollution. And bring me back to the same place four years from now and I will point at it as if we never left.

Condescending

Nails on the chalk board have never been so satisfying, comparing it to the words "I don't see you like that". I will gladly give up my own hearing so I can hear nothing else that would put me in this down that I can't seem to stand up from.

In the few seconds you were able to take me down without hesitation, it took you years to build with the most delicate brick that you said you made from the sentiment of your thoughts, having just anything to say wasn't how you did things.

Love was an eloquent demeaner that you made sure to focus on, and it steered you away from making the conscious effort of realizing that. Realizing that I just don't accept things like that.

Strawberries

They say the most

beautiful

things

are

like

when

strawberries

are

covered

in

dark

chocolate,

sweet with sweeter, but in this case bitter, bitter tasting. That is
what's left in my mouth when you left.

Flight DL1438

You're not,
You're not the person I have been looking for.
I thought it would be different.
I craved getting closer to the sun, just so I could feel the peace of
knowing you would be there.
The closeness of the seats, with the window slightly letting the silk
rays in didn't give me as much warmth as your hand when it was in
mine.

Give me a chance

When it's cold outside, I will be honest I feel like I need to belong.
To belong to a place where warmth is cherished.
Like a home with no walls and open like your embrace.
And when you touch my neck the goosebumps become your
fingertips.
And your touch continues as it brushes the heat emanating from my
skin, like the cold breeze that picks the surface of the snow pile.
Give me a chance and the motive to leave my eyes open when there is
nothing between me and your thoughts when they become like the
heavy rain that falls into the ocean.

It's complicated

As for me,

i

Love,

Love

so much.

And I think about how hard it will be to give it...

again.

I will see you soon

Thank you for all the light that you bring to someone else's life.

Thank you to the morning for waking you up today.

Thank you to the sun setting because after a long day I know I would spend it with you.

Thank you to Spanish guitars playing in romantic moments.

Thank you to the barista saving you from another brutal day.

Thank you for your constant inhales and your endless exhales, and to some it might seem "infuriating" but they are actually the sexiest sounds you can make.

Thank you to that soundtrack you listen to often that makes you love the path you're in, I hope you continue on that path regardless of the cloudy thoughts that form from anticipation.
Thank you, for coming into my life, without you I wouldn't have made it this far.

Conceptual lover

I will see you soon.
Whose fault is it?
Coffee....
And Love....

Sleep Paralysis

So, I woke up yesterday thinking that is was still the weekend.
I woke up a few minutes before my alarm clock which never happens.
I woke up to the pattering of rain on my roof, as if falling on my head,
putting me back to a sleepless position that I cannot break from.

The rain then falls against the window, as if battling the impenetrable
shield that keeps what's worse away.

My nightmares are back, fears that have no face and no emotion,
fears that fear nothing back and fears that become my best friends.

I scream, a haunting eternal scream that I am convinced anyone can
hear, instead it's a scream that becomes excruciating, but no one's
listening. I am not digging my nails in my neck, trying to search for a
voice, any voice that could save me from the insatiable fear of falling
further that the screams will have no choice but to be absorbed,
through my skin as I embody the fear that I cannot shake from.

My legs feel weightless
My arms swaying in the wind
My eyes roll back
My nose, with my nostrils expanding fighting, finding air, I feel no
oxygen
My hair with fingers pulling on my scalp
My stomach feels like I am being kicked with cleats

I am submerged, submerged in, submerged in a room with no light, no
door knob I was trained to find in a situation like this, nothing no
reason or motive to get up. A hand I feel a hand wrap around my lips,
I feel another hand slowly closing my neck, I am screaming, I want to
wake up if I am dreaming,

45

I watch myself walk to the fridge, I see my body staring at me, my body in front of the refrigerator light, I see my eyes glistening and a grin from me watching myself submerged.

I laugh, I feel like I am laughing, drowning and I can't swim, drowning and I can't help but to feel like I need to laugh to make sense of any of it.

I scream even though I tried it before,
I hear, a howl, no it's a run, and another, it's my alarm.
I am dreaming,
I am drowning, delusional disarray. Dominating, destroying my body.
I feel lifted, I feel like I am going to wake up.
My body in front of the refrigerator light, as if my savior slowly walks towards me, he will save me, lift my head up, encourage me and give me motives, reasons for my drowning.

Instead he grabs my neck, as if holding back my scream, my body wakes up in a cold sweat, with my alarms on for the 3rd time.
I am awake,
Except I still feel like I am drowning.

I talk to myself

I talk to myself often,

I talk about the subjects that I am afraid of confronting.

I talk about the unremitting thoughts that are unclear,

I talk about life as it should be, instead of how it is.

I talk about the dreams that haunt me, and the nightmares that make me better.

I talk about how confident I am about being alone.

I talk about the places that I want to visit.

I talk about the love that I always want to give.

I talk about the love that I already gave.

I talk about how love is abundant and no matter how much you think you waste it will always replenish itself.

I talk about how my mood changes within a span of an hour and I can't explain it with words.

I talk about listening more,

I talk about speaking less,

I talk about how insane it is that I have sleepless nights because creativity is crucial in the night time.

I talk about the moon and how it makes me think of the good times.

I talk about how conflicted I am when I want to nap.

I talk about how my mind is a blank canvas every morning.

I talk about how the images that I save in my memory is the paint for that canvas.

I talk about memories as if they are just people and not moments.

I talk about loving those memories unconditionally, even though they may have changed the way I look at myself.

I talk about all the things that I hold back.

I talk about how the things that I want to say, that I hold back are the pieces that I need to make myself complete.

I talk about my resilience and how that quality has always been one of my saviors.

I talk about the evenings and how romantic they would be if I had a partner to share it with.
I talk about how love is consistent,
I talk about love frequently,
I talk about love frequently that I forget how necessary it is to keep going.

I talk to myself,
I talk to myself, often.
So often that I can't help but to feel like it's the one thing that has allowed me to accept myself just the way I am.

Truth

I anticipate the truth,

I depend on it,

it's a way to feel complacent,

right now, I have come to this realization that I would prefer it above all.

Give me truth,

and I will give you comfort, I will make sure its tangible so you never let it go.

Give me the truth, your honest version of it and I will give you the relentless feeling of being centered.

A sensible undeniable stability that will carry your worries to no worries at all.

The truth, hand it to me, I deserve nothing more than to be submerged in all the words that I need to wake up tomorrow without that emptiness.

I want all of it, all the truth without the truth being a mirage in the scorching desert, walking to the oasis of truth, what I think is water to find more sand as I get closer as it appears in the distance again.

Give me truth,

Give me that before anything else.

Go easy

Your sincere compromise I couldn't recognize.

You whispered what seemed like pride in me but I couldn't feel it.

You told me my path after I created my own for decades.

My feet bleeding, I am satisfied, my mind seeping in my passionate beginnings.

My eyes lost in the grace of who I made proud.

My hands holding the most precious memories without you.

My love caressing my heart from the impurities you were supposed to save me from.

I couldn't recognize where you once stood, where you were revered to stand. You should have blocked the delicacy of the wind, and should have prevented the envy of the rain that came from the world from touching my skin. The world that is full of corruption, you should have covered my ears from the noise that you indulged in. Your hunger content, but never content for an unconditional love you were required to use for me.

I am content with your absence and quenched with the abundance of love in the places you were never a part of.

"L" word

Can I just start off by saying how brilliant I think your tongue is, you know that could be a compliment?

You hold back so much, you even hold back what you're meant to say, always afraid that the feedback and the response could be negative. Words that come from that tongue could be the demise and the realization that one can never let snowflakes fall on your tongue because it will mask the impact that you could have.

It's funny how you never think about the tongue until your about to describe all the things you can do with that tongue and you forget that you can't disclose any of it until your tongue moves in a speed allowing all the complication of words, those words getting you to that next step.

Sometimes I sit there in a dimmed room, because that's how I am able to absorb the day without letting any light in that might take away from the growth that I just made because I chose to wake up that morning.

That morning I woke up with my mouth swollen with words that I held back that night. That I could have said but my mind was ten steps behind. I know those words would have been a California forest fire that could spread and no ocean big enough could contain it.

I wanted to say the "L" word, it is not love, let me stop you from thinking that. I am lost, an "L" word that I am constantly feeling because when my emotions push me in every direction, pulling my limbs. And more importantly my heart strings, into a place I have never been, to that place you have always been.

I wanted nothing more than to tell you how constant you are and when you pull me out of the darkest breaches of my mind, I want nothing more than to give you all of my kindness, a kindness that I keep just for you, regardless of the condition of your mind, you always seem to appear.

51

Your battle wounds you experience like pomegranate seeds plucked by your mother. Her patience is like holding heavens doors and no one deserves it more than her baby.

Now you are healed and in a good place, while I try to figure out how to heal without allowing it to happen again. Even if you dropped bread crumbs, I will find my way back on my own because you never wanted me to follow.

Compilation,

Today, in the morning I have had the predisposition to feel better.
A forced composure, content, I think, but to my therapist or brother it
might be progress.

Progress, a word I am slightly terrified of, a word that makes me
wonder how far from normal I am and how progress might be a slight
shift in the wind, that may change my direction, but will lack the
placement that I need to feel like I am moving.
Moving from this spot I spend too much time in, a comfortable
command that I give myself.
A sufficient place, that I spend every moment of the day pleasing,
accepting this abusive relationship, that I am too deep to crawl out of.
A relationship that is spent where time is wasted on unnecessary
words, where I can't win an argument in my head, frustration turns
into anguish and I am suspended in a place that I cannot descend
from.
I have the sense to sense when it's not going good for me, like a
tension over my body, heavy weights over my eye lids and handcuffed
to a tethered chain to the rock of my past confidence.
When I say "I am almost there", out loud just loud enough for no one
to hear, it's because I am trying to convince myself that it will get
better.
A password to an account, I do not remember, a key made for a door
that does not exist, a pencil with no lead.
I am almost there.
That place that I thought would be better than this,
anything but this, a cloud of bliss in my mind and the rain drops are
memories I don't want to be drenched in.
I cannot wait to sleep tonight.

Realization:

Dear Snapchat

Dear Snapchat,

Stop reminding me of all the good times!

Sincerely,

-Someone that is trying to move on from the good times and into greater times.

You are human and you are built in years and destroyed in seconds.

You never think of it as a competition because you already feel defeated, you didn't lose and you never will lose.
I depend on you, I depend on you to show me that there is hope and I am able to find it and hold it because you made it tangible.

Enough

I hope this doesn't come off as an abstract thought,

but for you I would find the secret to stop time.

Hopefully I can make you feel like you are important enough.

In that still moment I would tell you how much your existence in my

life is enough.

More than enough.

Thanks

You will always hold a special place in my mind.

In my heart, you will never know how important your words were to my development.

In my soul, I cannot explain how at ease it has been to know that you are happy and more importantly your soul has rested.

Thank you.

Smile

I hate feeling like I haven't been enough for you.
The feeling that doubt and anxiety sit on your throat leaving no room
for the air intended for your breathing.
They make the greatest of friends, you know doubt and anxiety. They
prevent you from the formation of words. When in the same room
they command the time and have you exhausted from the energy that
you exert to keep your heavenly smile.

Keep your smile, it shouldn't be forced, smile because you allow it to
feed those who are starving from happiness.
Keep your smile because it could save the sun from dimming.

Keep your smile because I need your smile to know that everything is
going to be okay.
Keep your smile because I want to know it's that light from being in
that tunnel for too long.
Keep your smile because when you look in the mirror, I want it to give
you everything that you gave me.

Be yourself

How many times could you allow it?

What makes this time different than the many times before?

What allows you to keep going when the steps you keep taking burn the layers of your chest?

What's your motivation for feeling like you're under what isn't down anymore, but the weighted sadness that takes over the love for yourself?

What matters to you most?

How can you allow them to make you realize your perfection is closer to destruction?

How many times could you allow it?

How many times before you realize you're the most astonishing person I know.

Ramble

It may seem like I am rambling,

But I am not.
Sometimes the words that I say in the quiet place of my mind seem
profound and insatiable and when they come out of my mouth the
only word that comes out is "okay."
A word mediocre, a word that is used to agree with anything because
you just want whatever it is to end.
And just recently used to take the next step.

Next step, I know you're thinking it. Let's have this conversation
because we have never had it before. Next step to a decision or a path
you have yet to provoke. A peace that may seem toxic to others, but
for you, you're slowly decaying and the only feeling you get is picking
up heaven in your hands and taking a bite of it.

You think they are the foundation of youth, rejuvenation, and you
don't realize it is the poison slowly spreading or let's use another
word, coursing...coursing through your marrow not your
bloodstream...you see its much deeper than that.

I am going to ramble when it comes to you, I am going to keep going
until I am sure you understand the brilliance that I know you have,
don't act as if you have lost your mind. I give mine to you when I say
"okay".
It's to allow you to add any word that you prefer and what you hold
back or when you have nothing to say I will always continue to say
anything, just to keep you alive in my memories.

I will keep going

"There are things that I cannot change about myself"
Have you heard anyone say that but you never take those words
seriously because they come out of him or her or they so easily?
They point at the perfectly curved and strong nose as if they didn't
just paint a trunk with their index and thumb moving the exterior of
their nose like it weights as much as their self-doubt.
He hates the way his hair looks because its thinning into a miraculous
evolution, that he doesn't realize it is gifted to him to make him one
and in love his self-worth.
She hates the way her skin is oily and dry, at the same time her
coworker clogs her pores with the foundation on another foundation
that you know cracks and has flaws, and any second it can collapse in
the heat of her jealousy.
They hate the way their octaves are 1 to 2 pitches higher than the
next guy that thinks he is masculine, but he can barely breath from
the muscles that he builds because he says "I work out for myself"
knowing he isn't enough for himself. He works out to keep the dread
of his day from making him slow down.
And what about him, he hates the way his emotions control the very
moment he takes a bite and he can't stand the way his arm pits
profusely perspire of the overbearing voices in his head telling him he
isn't worth much.
Now I may not be in any room to talk about you, but if you would just
hear me out, I can tell you that I am confident in the next few words
and they will be everything that you need at this very moment. The
flaws that you cannot change are the ones that people overlook, your
smile makes this room look so dim, and those lines around your eyes
when I see your happiness are the lines that I need for this journey of
my life. When your eyes glisten, they promote a premonition that
everything is going to be alright. And those flared nostrils make my
passion bloom, like rain falling into a lake in the summertime.
Your smile makes me fall in love, with the snow even though it makes
me feel like I should say goodbye, one last time.

Your smile makes my thoughts turn, just like the pages that I can
write about you.
Your smile is everything to me.

\

Open arms

I prefer to share my thoughts with you.
I will share them under one condition and that condition is that you keep your arms wide open, what I am about to tell you will change the intention for those open arms.

Those open arms are what I need to make sense of why two cardinals on that tree branch have been sitting there observing me staring at me instead of having a conversation that could make a better tomorrow.

Don't change your intention and allow yourself to be drenched in these words that could change the hurricane winds, and create whirlpools of lust, and when it comes to a sleeping volcano, those words could erupt that volcano ten times with all the magnificence that you are.

Keep those open arms because the words that I might say could be sad and anxious. They don't encounter many ears, and when I know yours are listening, I will combat those thoughts in your head and I know I will win.

Keep your hands wide open and your body could be the vessel that embodies these words, making them finally be tangible and exquisite.

Now close your hands, and put them on your chest, your chest a cage for that palpitating hummingbird that wants to be imprisoned because it knows your desire and what your motivation is. Embrace these words, you have always been them, you have always been someone I look up to.

Love again

I have yet to understand why people feel the reason to put you down. Do they put you down because they're bored, are they mentally uncomfortable that they think the only way to leave the prison of their mind is to focus on the thing that you are questioning the most? The only validation they get is their very own or those brainwashed puppets they call their friends, and you know they're the ones that won't say a word until they are attached at the hip.

Don't ever question what it means to be loved because you are love. You have no idea with the love that is inside of you, that same love that makes a succulent plant nourished. That same love that flows inside of you can recover another person because you chose to donate blood. Your love can see tears stream down his face and you are able to wash your hands three times just so you make sure that everything will be okay. Your love is immense, that when anger fills to the point of overfill you are able to take it all away with the kindness of your breath.

Your love, is like music. Jazz music, an ensemble where the double bass is leading the rest of the band setting the mood for a night in the city. A jazz band with no structure, improvising the complex melodies of your heart because if there was sheet music it would sound perfect, and you know that you're more than that.

A serenade with a Spanish guitar, with your sweet range that you use to bribe with the different inflections, don't you know what it does to me.

Your love is the silence that I always seem to come back to, the quiet storm of what should be rhythm and blues, that sound I would consider every chance I get.

Butterflies in your stomach should never have to be turned to stone, instead let them be the gold that you are.

Do you know how necessary you are?

And then what?

You just delighted me, your eyes when they glisten in this light when your speaking in that voice all I want to do is hold myself.

And then what?

When I hold myself just like this and your eyes glisten back at me while I am looking at you recording with my iPhone, I say "and then what?"

When I stand here and I tell you exactly how I feel about your eyes glistening in this light and you tell me exactly how you feel and then say "and then what?" all I can do is tell you that I think I am falling in love with you.

But let's talk about, let's talk about how it started. As I kissed your knuckles, I kissed your palm first, I kissed your palm because I needed to show you how much I care about you...but you don't like that. You don't like the way I carried you and your misconceived confusion that is weight because you felt like something was missing.

And then what?

You never said a word that could have been what I needed to wake up from the cold sleepless nights that I could have been resting. Sleep never met me in the night.

And then what?

Your eyes constantly avoided my gaze, and when I wanted you to look, no camera could capture your perfection, you looked the other way, you were afraid to fall deeper than you already have.

And then what?

The questions that I had answers to, that you could have asked in any way you wanted, were questions that I thought about and they ate me from inside, all I wanted was for you to listen.

And then what?

Let's go back to sleepless nights. You pushed me away. Let's talk about it, you know I realized at a Coney Island at 3:09am and we were saying "and then what?". It was a red turbine, a red shirt, a red jacket, red pants and white shoes...then it was a Michigan salad with cranberries, pickled onions, lettuce, tangerines, black olives and possibly some raisins I am not sure, and the fries, with a Pepsi. And it started with "and then what?", and we tried to figure out where it was going and twelve minutes later, we figured that it would begin with "and then what" and end with "and then what" because there is no before and after.

And then what?

We could say "and then what?" and keep going and talk about the same things that bothered us yesterday and instead we can say "and then what? "and continue from there and realize that we had the answer all along, we are blinded by the infatuation that comes from the sadness that we crave because it's better to feel something then nothing at all.

And then what?

I can deliver a message to you, and I wouldn't wait for that response because I am not sure that you will reply. Making me wait in that quiet place for you is your way of showing me how torturing me is more important than telling me the truth.

And then what?

And I sit in a good place that I have spent time building from the shattered pieces that you created because that's the only way I can create a foundation for my emotions stronger than I have ever had before. A glass palace, with a maze entrance that I have made, every step that will be taken will be the step suitable for the vast greatness that I will become. With ceilings that have no limits and no indication of what could be from the time that I know will be my ultimate healer.

And then what?

When I say that I can keep going, and I can create more words to describe what cycle my depression could put me in. I have yet to figure out its obsession with me. Why does it weigh me down and prevent me from flying to a higher ground that has the air that I need to inhale? Why does it crave my time and why does it allow me to travel the woods without any sense of building a camp fire because preferring the cold wet ground is expected over making a crisp fire that could go against the battles in my head trying to convince me how good I am at not being enough?

And then what?

Realization

I feel like this discussion is overdue,
Like we should have had told each other where we hide the rocks that
we collected at every destination in what I considered our love, in the
secret place that we only knew about.
Remember that day, it was the evening and the sun descended behind
the purple horizon and the thought of you walking beside me on a
beach, where the sand erases our progress, but walking on that beach
was what I wanted regardless.
Constellations, in the sky were not familiar figures in the night,
instead the stars formed a dome of lights above us, surrounding us
with a terror of what tomorrow might bring. We sat in that dome
while the wind shuffled our feelings as if we picked subjects from a
hat.
And then it happened...the rocks that we collected from the places we
called love became the rocks that I felt I was being stoned with,
exposing the decaying flesh that I have been covering up with what I
thought was my position in your life.
Walking on the beach, where there would never be a sunset, but a
hurricane, hurricane winds that would leave me in the confusion that
I am still in. In a place where my mind can only associate the ocean
with the trauma of the truth that I had to figure out on my own.
The night sky and the constellations haven't formed around me, in a
dome the way it did before you left. Instead, they form a cage,
suffocating, suffocating the bird that is inside of me preventing it from
expanding, from the dystrophia that is the collection of love that I
should have preserved for myself. And every day the cage walls grow
smaller.
You said "I feel like this discussion is overdue", as if this discussion
has a limit, or the shit that I feel inside have a deadline. Where I am
forced to just feel like I have no voice, and if I shouldn't be responsible
for the shit that I feel inside. They are my emotions, right? I created
them, just like my body rushes blood to my brain to help me survive

68

this thing called...love, or however it is defined in whatever words that you use to make yourself feel better.

My mind

I knew I walked into an uncomfortable position when I can no longer make up complete sentences.

My mind lost all meaning for words, syntax and direction and all I can do is look toward the closest wall in order to feel some sort of stability. You may ask yourself how a wall could give closure or the incessant idea of being in a heavenly place, but it does.

It actually allows all of my fears, preconceived notions about anything and the allowance to be decent. I know what would be behind me if I needed to back up into it.

That wall is the only way I could win a battle, a battle of manipulation, a battle where the weapons are not physically harmful and will not end my life.

It's a battle of words, comprised and full of structure that can either build more defenses or tear down the fragile barricades that make up my mind.

With delicacy I have no room to look further into a conversation where my mind can freeze time just long enough to allow access to a better understanding of what you desire.

What do you desire?

What do you want most outside of expatriation or decay?

I will tell you what I want, selfishly after I just asked you a question, I want truth, a better understanding of how well you listened to all the words that just came out of me, that I built and spent time forming in order for you to better understand me.

"Do you love me back?"

I want then an answer, and the answer should start off with the question that I presented to you and if it doesn't begin with that then I know how much you never wanted to listen.

Because of that wall I have all the understanding that I need and the support that I depended on all this time.

Rest

Rest has been a battle that I have been facing.

Facing now more than I have ever faced before.

There was a reason for that night, that war that nobody won.

There was a reason for the moments that words were exchanged and the exhale of your breathing seems more vicious than the words that were coming out of your mouth.

Could I allow my mind to rest, in this rose petal coffin full of the words from a chapter book I would rather be submerged into.

Sleep, just so I can sleep and rest the eyes that can't seem to stop their repeating of batting, they are trying to hold back the water behind a dam that's just been holding on for too long.

Rest has been a battle that I have been facing.

Like my eyelids need permission to flutter when they are simply moving because my kindness has always been stronger than my need to be cruel to your eye lids, I refuse to hurt you the way you keep hurting me.

Can I ask you something?

Do you ask for permission to blink your eyes, like how a period stops a sentence and completes the thought that has a purpose?

How after every phrase that makes its way from your mouth has a slight echo that enters my ears and makes my body shiver all over in paralysis?

I want you happy!

Is that so crazy to say even though I know you don't think about me.

I want you to look at the ground and be content with your placement and when you look back, that is if you look back, I want you to look at the footsteps in the sand and be comfortable enough to take another step without having to worry about the ocean taking them away.

When you look at the night sky, I want the moon to be your best friend and not the thing associated with the love that you know you had, that you know could have been the only thing sure. And you would be more than okay with that.

The trails that many could have taken but those many have never taken it with you, could have been trails that could have led us to the epitome of love. To the place where you could access only when you are sitting with love in front of a camp fire, and the frail fingers lock into your frail fingers sitting in silence because that moment is more precious than anytime where your fingers had no limits.

Ink, the ink that soaked those countless pages. And the pages that were once acres of trees were words that I could have equaled to being the best words that could have been quotes that would eventually be posted just so others that view that post could understand the exact feeling that just sits on the tip of my tongue, and then when asked, the simple response of "oh, it's just a quote", hoping anyone would believe it.

Time, made it all clear. It made us realize that love is abundant, an infinite well that could never be dry, that could never be tainted or wasted. If that love was the only thing left in a home that was broken after countless years, love would be the indestructible glue that could have held it all together.

I write, I write words down hoping I could make sense of the thoughts that take over my head like when I drive to a place, I park and I don't even remember that I made a left, right, left, left, right, right, right and another right to make it to that place that I claimed as my home.

I think my mind forgot itself at the door. That's what happened, my mind forgot itself at the door and when it came down to it, love welcomed my heart in a warm caress and the only thing my mind could do is watch from the outside, watching the happiness that I never could have gained from anyone else except myself. Watching love intertwine in laughter and the subtle sounds of English artists, to watching petals decay in a candle polluted room. Where the heat of your body was warmer than any blanket.

I want you to be happy!
I want you to experience the things that I lacked. I want you to run as fast as your lungs allow not from the things that scare you but towards the things you love most. I want you to keep attempting to fly, fly as high and as far as you can. And beyond that point. With your hands, hold what it is that tells you that you're important, not to them but how important you are for this world because if this world had more people like you, this world would be envious of itself.

I want you to be happy, I want you to be yourself.

Dodge Park

Dear October,

Your rain seems endless.

When the temperature is evident by breathing.

That bridge that took you to where you want to be, lost, the divide between where I am and where I would like to end up.

How the dead leaves scream back to life when you step on them.

I don't think about it.

Or rather I try to forget about you there under the umbrella.

Walking away.

In the evening

I thought about you yesterday
I thought about you a little more than usual.
I thought about your smile and how I want to see it again.
I really want to see your smile,
again.

Broken

I am sometimes fascinated by the things that make sense to me.
You're right, I am broken

But who can decide that,
who can decide when you feel the need to search for water at what
seems like days even though it's a few seconds away in the middle of
the night?

But no, you're right I am broken

I am broken when I say I would rather stay awake a little longer
because writing this poem is more important to me then falling asleep
when I have to fight to stay awake the next day, that is a challenge
that I will gladly accept.

But maybe you're right, I am broken

Just like the frame that was made for the pictures, my frames are full
of words, simple sentences that I could have written in my hand
writing but I used a type writer because the aesthetic makes me value
my words so much more.

You're right, I am broken

I can feel the blood flow through my bloodstream, like fire, walking
into any place with perfectly folded clothes still isn't good enough in
my eyes.

But you're right, I am broken

My voice shakes and trembles at the thought of entering a place with
more faces then all of mine. And as if smiling is enough and constantly
feeling disgust inside isn't enough to allow me to leave.

But you're right, I am broken

I am broken enough to realize that when I see someone cry for hurting
someone else, I can't help but to feel more sympathy for them then
the person they hurt because any tear shed is enough to make me feel
the same feeling I have when I watch any movie where there is a
father present in their child's life.

But you're right I am broken

I am broken enough to bask in the rain while shunning the sun.

You're right I am broken

I am broken with good intention, my cracked facial expressions and
harmonious voice with the other voices in my head are a choir for
your benefit. I am broken with bad intention because my mind will

take me to places deeper than the surface, I am broken because
instead of blaming myself, I blame my mind as if it's another person
waiting for me to slip just the slightest so it can scold me when we're
the only two in the room.

You're right I am broken

I am broken enough to realize that drinking coffee black makes me a
psychopath based off of that 10th article I read on coffee because
doing my homework when it's due in 10 minutes isn't as important.

You're right though, I am broken

I am broken,
you're right, but at least I am doing something about it, what are you
doing about it?

Last time

I told myself a year ago that I would be in a happier place,
I also told myself that I would get over you.
This year I am in a happier place, except I am not over,
You.

Sometimes

At some point you are going to realize how important you are,
when that happens, nothing will be more important than your
happiness.

Conversations

I miss the conversations we had,
the exceptional exhaustion, and no matter how tired and forgetful I
didn't ever forget those conversations.
Conversations about growth and content cultivating attitude that
form from all of this exhaustion will come the progress that you want
nothing but to embody.

A collection of words that seep into your skin, inflections of the voice
rushing blood streams, I am full of love.
Full of love, I am making,
Forming impulsive words like leaves in the rainy autumn day in a
rushing river so that conversation can reach the oceans.

Conversations that heighten senses, sensual solitude only with you I
want those conversations to be heard by the world.
The world being you, you embrace these conversations as if they are
crucial to living lavishly in the ballroom of your mind, I have more
conversations, endless conversations that I want nothing more but for
you to be involved so that I can be the sense that never makes sense
in a story.

I live here in this moment, when a conversation that I had with you
was the one thing that I looked forward to,
I miss the conversations we had,
I miss them being part of my day.

Closer

When your kindness is breached by the cruelty of their words.
That's when you should walk away.

Air

I saw your picture yesterday
It made me smile, it made me realize how good I had it.
How good it felt to be part of your space.
How good it felt to breath the same air and despite the quiet moments
that air connected us.

That air had our thoughts clash when we disagreed and mended our
thoughts when we agreed with each other.
The air made us one with nature, as if the grass underneath us
voluntarily grew to cushion the heaviness of our love so we always
knew we had support.

That air sent butterflies to our stomachs, when we first met, without
that air, my "hey" and your "hello" would have never faced one
another.

That air sent a surge down my spine, so divine that I felt god engulf
me in a ray of everything that is great, made the turbines of my lungs
expand and that made its way to my chest, palpating my heart so I
know how important you are to my everyday moments.

Fingertips, that air between my fingertips felt as dense as rain when it
falls unintentionally on the thick windshield on my car on a Saturday
night, not allowing the density from that rain to ruin your plans.

That air, sits in the seat that you were obligated to leave because you
have to wake up the next morning, setting your 10 alarm clocks
knowing you're only going to get up for the last one.

That air makes flower petals wisp through the air and when they fall,
they fall exactly the way it's supposed to be, as they are scattered to
take up the space that's intended for them.

That air makes fire bloom, makes fire on the surface of water, so beautiful as elements blend in all the ways arms can hold other arms in all the right positions.
That air makes airplanes that weight in tons lift from the ground and into the sky as if they are full of helium.

But....

When that air suffocated me, as if your palms made contact with my brave lips. So, brave they didn't hold back, they didn't hold back the privileges that they had before they made contact.

Air engulfed the space that you felt a void, barely containing I, my air unraveled your demons from the past that didn't sit well with you.

Without my air, I could not bear to take a step towards what I thought was the right direction. As a guiding light in a cave full of stalactites that are my flaws, that I could use to guide me but instead I depend on the light that I am incapable of making.

That air the one that surrounds me guiding my hips into the next footstep allows me to love this world even though this world needs more air to breath properly.

My air is independent when it's alone, but when you step towards me in the coldest composure, I know my air will make you melt. Melt into the person that you want to be, because my air allows you to feel invincible.

My air is igniting, without my air fire would be to cowardice, it wouldn't even show up in desperation.
My air is constant, my air compromises and commemorates your inhales because my air is dense.
My air makes mosquitos hover around skin full of the tired sweat on your lip, my air is miraculous, its senile, my air makes flowers bloom, pollinated like forced dew drops in the summer morning.

My air is finesse, its powerful, my air is unruly, it is a chained lion forced to watch other lions eat.

My air is complicated, it is a window cracked open in a winter night, a whisper that doesn't travel, my air is a broken wing on an ostrich, a war that nobody wins. A collection of photo albums in a house fire, my air is cold, it is a word that has no meaning. My air is the moon when you are not able to see it in the night.

My air is always there, it has always been here and you chose to hold your breath.

Almost

I
want
to tell,
that
I
Am
okay,
I
promise

Fervid Lips

And when it came to knowledge,
I gladly accepted being a coward, I knew that it was the first step to
facing the truth.

Find me

Accept this state of mind.
You will be forced to make it your first home.

Beginning

Sit in silence,

that's the best way to figure out all of the noise.

This is for all the thoughts that never made sense, this is for the feelings that cannot be explained in a different perspective, this is for you, it has always been for you, so I thank you, for being the reason that words cannot be comprised without the confusion that you have in your mind.

Sincerely,
-Someone that tries to explain "it" with words

Ali Al-Arithy is a Detroit based poet and an educator that was born in a refugee camp in Saudi Arabia. His other collection of poems from his first book *Safe:* was released in 2018. The subjects that he writes about are related to mental health, loss, reflection, capability, dependence on oneself and acceptance. He is a graduate from the University of Michigan-Dearborn and pursuing his masters in Creative Writing at Eastern Michigan University.